Be Clear Now!

A BEGINNERS GUIDE TO PENDULUM CLEARING

Brian T Roberts

Minister of Light and Sound

AyniWrite Press, Albuquerque, NM

For more Information or free PDF files of the Be Clear Now and *I AM* Charts Contact the author or:
AyniWrite Press, Albuquerque, NM
http://ayniwritepress.com

Printed in the United States of America

Edited by Carole Conlon
Book Cover Art "The Lion Goddess" by Karin Couture
http://lifeseedcodes.com

Be Clear Now! A Beginner's Guide to Pendulum Clearing / Roberts – 1st Edition
ISBN 978-0-9984624-0-0

Table of Contents

Be sure to DOWNLOAD YOUR *FREE* PDF files of the full color
Be Clear Now and *I AM* charts now.
Details on page 44

Author's Preface

Life's journey is an ever-deepening spiral that leads to the light. The closer you arrive to that "Presence" of your own *I AM Being*," the more and greater the desire to help humanity move into the light of "Being and Knowing" and clarity.

As I worked on the Be Clear Now project as part of my life's journey, I thought that it would be catalytic and humbling to consult the I Ching, a Chinese divination method. The interpretation of that reading was truly amazing. Its wisdom seemed to apply not only to those of us researching and creating the project, but also to those already on board and even to any who will join us at a future date. I applaud those who have made it this far; welcome and thank you for being.

Those of you who have never heard of the I Ching or consulted it in any way, may be informed that Confucius said on his death bed, that he wished he had discovered it earlier in his life. The origin of the Oracle or Book of Changes remains hidden. All we know is that it was in use 1100 years before Christ.

The question that I put forward to the I Ching was "What is the reality of this work, Be Clear Now?" The reading produced an initial hexagram with 2 changing lines which resulted in the 2nd hexagram.

The first hexagram was number 12 Standstill (Stagnation)

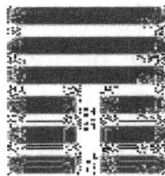

The Judgment: *Standstill, people do not further*. (The question here is "Are people ready ?")

The lines were 9 in the 4th place reading: *He who acts at the command of the highest, remains without blame*. Those of like mind partake of the blessing.

The line 9 in the 6th place reads: *The Standstill comes to an end. First Standstill, then good fortune*.

This brings us to the hexagram Pi/Number 8 "Holding Together": *The waters on the surface come together like an ocean where all the rivers come together.*

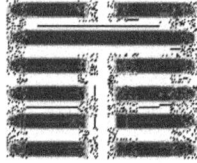

The Judgment: Holding Together brings good fortune. Inquire of the Oracle again whether you possess sublimity, constancy and perseverance. (I also interpret this to mean keep clearing.)
There is no blame and people who are uncertain gradually join in.
The Image: On the earth the image of HOLDING TOGETHER. Thus the kings of antiquity bestowed the different states as fiefs and cultivated friendly relations with the feudal lords.

So moving forward it now seems is the result of years of preparation but more importantly probably the timing is right. Or as Lao Tsu said in the Tao Te Ching, "The highest good is like water. Water gives life to the 10 thousand things and does not strive. It flows in places men reject and so it is like the Tao.

In dwelling, be close to the land.
In meditation, go deep in the heart.
In speech, be true.
In ruling, be just.
In business, be competent.
In action, watch the timing.

Blessings on your journey,
Brian T Roberts

Acknowledgments

It has been a great pleasure for me to help synergize this dowsing/ clearing/ beginner's work with the charts. This has only been made possible by the great work of Carole Conlon and some of her support team including Barbara Rose.

I am also grateful to my partner Karin Couture for her contribution of the cover art, but also for her tremendous efforts to learn the system which has kept us fresh and enthusiastic.

Introduction

If imitation was the highest form of flattery, then that explains why I think that Carole Conlon's work developing the LifeWeaving system and dowsing charts is simply superb. I do not think that there is any other system out in the market quite like it. If so, I would love to see it. I really wish more people would appreciate and get along with LifeWeaving. Ah, but just maybe it is a little tricky getting started. This is why, with Carole's support, I volunteered to organize a start chart, a beginner's chart. I have combined elements from a few other charts with some of the wisdom of Carole's LifeWeaving, but just the very basics.

Be Clear Now! is not a perfect work but it's a good start, and I promise to get student feedback to continue to evolve it. Training and teaching are like a spiral where one is always learning and delving deeper into the mysteries of life, energy, relationships and clarity. I've tried, cried and asked myself why? All I get is that this has been a good thing to do, to apply the principles at a basic level. I hope it helps you. I have trained dowsing students and watched them do great things. This is my motivation.

This is a basic and introductory level and it is my suggestion that once you are ready, move on to Carole's books and LifeWeaving charts for advanced training.

I suppose that everyone who attempts to dowse will first of all have to understand dowsing is a little bit Zen. Naturally everyone can do it. But natural and normal are still just getting acquainted with one another on the planet. Dowsing involves concentration, relaxation, inspiration and a focused sense of inquiry. You do not dowse like you drive a car. People can drive a car while smoking a cigarette, listening to the radio, talking on a cell phone while booking a table at a restaurant, wondering what to wear while imagining what their date will be wearing. Dowsing is NOT a multi-tasking process. It is very Zen. It's natural. No one can explain it. It is like riding a bicycle. You either have it or not. Is it like hearing, seeing, smelling, tasting, touching? No probably not. It is more like riding a bicycle. You try and try, try and fail, but then you get it. Dowsing is the same thing. You let go of control and then something kinesthetic slips in. Suddenly your conscious, subconscious and superconscious minds all align and a simple thing like Yes, No, or Neutral happens. It's magic. No, it's natural, and, yes, it's dowsing.

There are a number of dowsing books that deal with finding water, oil, gold, treasure, artifacts, wealth and fortune. This is not that book/chart. Here we are dealing with the anatomy of the spirit and chakras, subtle energies, light and shadow energies, cords, emotions, influences and protection.

These are a few examples of clearing: A person, presently working in a specific field and very knowledgeable about the topic, is having a problem with a college professor because that student is better informed than the professor. This leads to problems between the professor and the student who wants to obtain the degree. Clear them and see that they both can move on amicably. Or a case where a person has taken a physical exam and already failed twice, only one last chance. Clear him and observe that the third time is a charm; he passes. Is this magic? No. The act of clearing puts unseen forces or energy into motion. One may observe the physical effects of wind on the water. You can ride the wind but you just can't see it.

You look at your umbrella before leaving the house. The weather is clear outside right now but you check. You take your pendulum out, get a positive response and decide to take that umbrella. Forty-five minutes later you exit the train station and no, you will not be walking in the rain. You have an umbrella. Or one day you have a few hours to kill so you decide to check out the movies. Your Higher Self knows what you like so you use a numbering system on your left hand, two points per finger. You question when you get a 10 on a movie with an actress you do not really like, or prefer but you go anyway and oh what a pleasant surprise, a great movie. It's magic. No, it's dowsing.

My favorite cord clearing story: I received a call from David S. and a request for clearing. Since he was driving in his car, I suggested that he continue to his destination and that I would clear him and send him a text with my result of findings. He had quite a few cords, some attached to his alta major chakra at the back of his neck. His cords were cleared and I sent a text. He called me back later and expressed his amazement because the previous day he had purchased some heavy-duty dandruff shampoo because, as he explained, the "itch" at the back of his neck was driving him crazy. Once he was cleared, the itching stopped; scout's honor.

Everyone has a Zen mind, an intuitive mind, a neo-cortex of the brain, the mind of the Buddha, but you have to find it to use this. If truth would be told the whole world is living a lie, which some folks think is okay as long as their teeth are white. It appears more of an animal kingdom that a Hu-man kingdom. It has lost the *I AM* Code. Do you know the difference between the personality and individuality? The answer is everything! There is only One Being and we are all part of it. There is only One Mind and we are all using this. In essence, we may all be One. As a personality we are simply a projection machine and the collective distortions are causing the world in/of chaos. Can we live in the world and not be of it? We can try!

You could be different, know the difference between fact and fiction, between the truth and the lie. You most definitely can find out. Why? Because it is your God-given gift to feel what is in the wind, to look out and see the stars and to chart a course, to be "I AM Guided". The Be Clear Now method will help you dial this in.

Five hundred years ago most people could not read. Today most people do not dowse. Be the first one in your family to turn out sane and happy, or at least moderately content and well directed. Life is a challenge - rise up to meet it. The poet Rumi says if you are walking through a graveyard, if you see a spook run towards it. I personally do not walk through graveyards but I have met a few persons who have spooks, kooks, discarnates (ghosts) or entities and a volume of toxic waste in their subtle energy field.

Have you been to any airports lately? This is not a good place to dowse because of the large number of people constantly moving around. Everyone has a guardian angel and everyone who flies has an angel that says, "I'll see you on the other side'. Do not dowse in an airport. Instead call a dowsing buddy for help. There are people and places and things that need to be cleared, or to be avoided. Allow me to teach you how to do this and then you can start to increase the miracles in your life!

May the full force of "Be Clear Now" be upon you, now and always,
Brian T Roberts

P.S. If not, call me right away at 206.799.5605!

[1]

Clearing, What is It?

All living things emit energy and have a surrounding field of living energy. These fields are electric (E) and magnetic (M). Without the planet's EM field the ultraviolet rays emitted by the sun would burn and destroy us. Additionally there are several other invisible things that are having a deep influence on your life right now: planets, the sun, the moon, the past, people's expectations about the future, emotions, other people's stuff, relationships, cellular memory, energetic cords attached to us, soul programs, thought forms and perceptions, world chaos, the weather − all factors impacting us. Luckily we can clear the negative influences to a high degree. How is this possible? When we send an energetic wave at another identical wave, the energy matches it in reverse and thereby they cancel each other out. This effect can happen in many different ways when using tuning forks, amplifiers or even the voice.

Clearing can also happen in a surprising way. My dowsing teacher, Carole Conlon (who is also an acupuncturist), was sharing with me that she would ask people what their complaints were. One person complaining of headaches, intestinal disorders and sciatica also tested with chakra imbalances and entities and attached energetic cords. After clearing these entities, cords and balancing the chakras, the headache, intestinal and back problems cleared up. At that point the session was done.

When doing clearing work, you can also help people who are at another location. Most of the work I do these days is long distance.

One day I was scheduled to meet with a friend, a health care professional, and she had to cancel our date as she was sick. I asked her if I could do a clearing on her. We were talking on the phone, mind you. She said what? I said a clearing. She said yes. So I checked in *"May I? Can I? Should I?"* and got a *"yes."* I proceeded to recite the

Invocation on the chart and began my questions, found the influences affecting her, took them to the Clearing Macro to release them and completed the clearing. One hour later she called me and said "I do not know what you did but I am walking around my apartment singing to my cat." It turned out that this friend's parents were sending a lot of cords that were attaching to her and draining her energy.

That great visionary Edgar Cayce said that "Unseen forces are greater than the seen." Practitioners can acquire a great many cords because desperate people - who may otherwise be good in nature - cling to their health care providers (or others) who have healthier bodies or minds. However, these cords are too many to wear without damage to the recipient.

Let's learn to clear them.

Clearing often works in two stages - 1) Clear, and 2) Activate. However for some sessions I am limited for time and all I can do is clear entities off a person. Normally however I start with the Be Clear Now chart or some of the LifeWeaving charts and finish with the *I AM* chart.

What a clearing consists of:
a) Ask for permission, *"May I? Can I? Should I?"*
b) Bring in the light by using the Invocation
c) Go through the sections on the Be Clear Now chart to find the influences
d) Bring what you find to the Clearing Macro and recite the mantra and completion check.

The method is wonderful and easy once you learn how to do this clearing work. It is a necessary tool for self maintenance and a great tool to help transform yourself, clients, friends and family.

Recently my partner, Karin, was doing work for a young woman over a period of thirty days. Among the woman's problems were entity attachments. When next we met with the woman's mother, she told us that her daughter was totally transformed. Fortunately the mother is now in the process of learning to dowse and do the clearing work. God save the King! I mean, God save the Queen!

Done well, dowsing/clearing work will open up new worlds for you.

Programming Your Pendulum

Webster defines a program as "a plan or system under which action may be taken towards a goal". The purpose of programming, to achieve maximum accuracy, is done by establishing with your dowsing system, in this case your pendulum, some mutually acceptable, pre-established, agreements and understandings about words, phrases, conditions and what is meant by different pendulum movements. If working with charts, you must program your pendulum to follow directions on the chart, even if those directions are different from your norm.

When working with the Be Clear Now and *I AM* charts, part of the programming is to 'teach' your pendulum to return to the neutral line after all options on that particular chart or section have been found. This allows the dowser to know to return to the Chart Key for more information.

The most basic form of programming in dowsing is establishing "agreed upon" conditions such as what motion indicates a 'yes' and what indicates 'no'.

Establishing Yes and No Answers

Step 1. Relax, become quiet and drift into a prayerful mood (alpha state).

Step 2. Take your pendulum and hold the string or chain between your thumb and first finger with about 1-1/2 to 3 inches string length. The length determines how fast it will swing so find the best length for you.

Step 3. Holding the pendulum over the center of the chart, manually (by gently moving your hand and fingers) make the pendulum start swinging towards the "YES" and ask and expect it to keep swinging on its own without your help. Ask it out loud, with about the same normal speaking voice and tone as talking to a person. If it stops, start it over again, ask it to keep going. Watch only the 'leading edge', the upper or forward half of the pendulum's swing, and ignore the other half, from the midpoint of the swing and back towards you. Repeat until the pendulum keeps swinging on its own. You will be deliberately starting the pendulum and then asking it to keep swinging with no additional help from you. You are simply training your system to react in a predetermined way.

Step 4. Return the pendulum to neutral in front of you by gently restricting its motion and putting it back into a gentle neutral swing.

Step 5. Repeat Step 3 to obtain the "NO" response and ingrain that pattern. Your fingers are still over the center of the circle and you are ignoring one half of the swing.

Step 6. Once the pendulum is swinging by itself to the "NO" circle on the chart, ask it, while it is still swinging, to work its way clockwise back to "YES" and then continue to the "Ready Diamond."

Step 7. Next ask it to work its way clockwise from the "Ready" to "YES," then counter-clockwise back to the "NO", and then clockwise back to the "YES". Practice Steps 5, 6 and 7 several times until your pendulum easily navigates the yes and no circles on the chart.

Step 8. Practice using the chart by asking simple yes and no questions that you know the answers to. For example: "Was I born in ____ state?" "Is my name Mickey Mouse?" "Am I married?"

Note that once you input programs into the dowsing system you DO NOT have to repeat the programming each time you dowse. They are automatically and continually in effect until changed by you.

Other Things to Be Aware of

The following are just a few important things to remember that will make you a superb dowser:

- Do pendulum testing when you are feeling fresh and relaxed in a quiet and comfortable area free of interruptions and distractions.
- Be neutral about expected answers. If you need to check sensitive information (like health issues on yourself or someone close to you), either find a 'pendulum buddy' to do the testing or at least have them check your answers for accuracy.

- Please, no "*Should I?*" questions. Instead ask a question like *"What level is in effect for my question?"* or, *"What does this calibrate?"* For example, *"What is the calibration for my enjoying one beer?"* The response might be positive. However, if you ask *"What is the level for drinking 10 beers?"* your answer will most likely be negative. You can still drink 10 beers but do not drive and do expect a bad hangover to result. You divine and then decide.

- Often a dowser asks a question like *"Does it calibrate higher to take class A or class B?"* Note that your first question should actually be *"Does it calibrate for me to take a class at this time?"* Remember to start your questions at the beginning!

Breathe in Awareness Exercise

A special exercise to help you prepare for dowsing is <u>Breathe in Awareness</u>: The world breathes on a scale or rhythm of 3 and perhaps this represents the lower chakras. Instead, exercise by breathing in to the count of 4, hold to the count of 4, exhale to the count of 4. Repeat 4 times. Take note of what you notice. Do this as often as you can, anywhere, anytime.

Presenting the Be Clear Now Chart

Proceed in Awareness by Asking Permission

Ask, seek and knock, always, by using the *Invocation* and asking to bring in the Light. Seek permission always, *"May I?, Can I?, Should I?"*, before doing any inquiry. Only now with permission are we able to knock at the door of understanding. If you will use all the invocations, the *I AM*, Violet Flame and Great Invocation, you will attract guides that are aligned with the Divine Plan, pure and simple.

Ask is the turn inside.
Seek is the sensitization to Soul clarity/energy.
Knock is our bended knee and the coming with humility
to participate in the Divine Plan, free of astral influences,
clear of pesky human disadvantages,
aligning our chakras with Source.

Gently swing the pendulum over the chart at the Balance (Neutral) section and ask *"May I? Can I? Should I?"* Yes means go. No means No.

Elements of the Be Clear Now Chart

Ready: Your pendulum should move to the Ready Diamond should test after doing the invocation and obtaining permission to work on someone. This is your okay to begin dowsing.

A 1 Hitchhikers ...Cords...
Chakras

B 1 Electrical Energy ...
Including Meridians and
Related Circuitry

2 Aura...Weak, Leaks,
Damaged, Levels, Prana

3 Chakras...Balance, Color,
Size, Shape

4 Vitality... Qi, Yin, Yang, Prana, Life Energies, Love

5 Shadow Energies... Home,
Workplace, Other Space,
Travel Places

6 Vitamins...A, B, C, D, E

C 1 Mental...Control, Energies,
Function, Balance, Stability,
Projections

2 Emotion...Hormone, Environment, Substances (food,
medicines, stimulants, etc.)

3 Image...Attitude about Life,
People, World, Self, Success,
Health

4 Programs...Patterns, Mindsets, Habits, Traits, Culture,
Ancestral, Past Lives

5 Nervous System...Stress,
Defects, Genetic, Energetic

6 Chaos...Vibrations, Environment, Persons, Oppressions,
Pressures

C 8 Cords...Inbound or Attachments by others, Chakras or
Anatomy

9 Ancestral...Past Life, Effects,
Entanglements, Attachments,
Karma

10 Hitchhikers...Astral Energies
or Beings, Interfering,
Obstructing

11 Influences...Combinations of
Psychic, Emotional, Mental,
Entanglements, Astral
Entities, Karma, Environment

12 Protection...Weakness of
Physical, Mental, Psychic,
Astral, Aura, Influences,
Energies, Forces, etc.

D 1 Ions and Electrolytes

2 Amino Acids...levels, balance

3 Acid/Alkaline Balance

4 Toxins

5 Infection

6 Allergies...plant, animal,
chemical, mental, emotional,
psychic...

7 Systems...Digestion, Circulation, Immune, Hormone,
Enzyme, Communication, etc.

8 Discomfort...Pain, Warning,
Physical, Mental, Psychic,
Spiritual, Astral

F Activities

1 CLEARING   7 PLAY
2 CEREMONY   8 RELAX
3 EAT   9 SLEEP
4 EXERCISE   10 STUDY
5 MAINTENANCE 11 WORK
6 MEDITATION 12 OTHER

G Seven
Chakras

1 Crown   5 Solar Plexus
2 Brow   6 Abdominal
3 Throat   7 Root
4 Heart

NO   YES

WHITE FLAG

Clearing Macro

Completion Check

Is the issue   Is the issue
clear for the   clear on all
                   levels:
Trinity:
The Ego?   Physical?
The Self   Energetic?
The Soul   Emotional?
Assigned   Mental?
spiritual   Spiritual?

REV'D 19 2016

The Be Clear Now Chart

Balance: Balance is a state of neutrality often represented by the powerful Yin/Yang symbol. You could meditate on this symbol for years because it represents the two primary forces in the universe: yin/yang, expansion/contraction, male/female, negative and positive, light/dark. The I Ching says that everything in the universe is in flux, moving towards the center or the periphery. The only thing that is constant is change and dowsing gives us a visual of its direction, speed, timing and fluidity.

No and Yes: Here we have the left side of the chart as negative/no, and on the right side positive/yes. Some charts reverse this. As long as you are clear and you have programmed the pendulum to this chart, all will be good.

For our purpose we need to have a word symbol for what is empowering, for what adds to us; the word is *positive*. What takes away or diminishes us is towards negative. However, they are not absolutes but mirrors in the flux of the field. No/Negative is not always a bad response and Yes/Positive is not always good. For example: if you find yourself having a pain radiating down your left arm and dowse to see if you are having a heart attack, you might get a negative. Well that's good. Always remember that common sense is the groundwork for any type of intuitive work.

Red Flag: If the red flag tests, it informs you that some situations and questions may be outside your zone of inclusion, your dowsing ability at this stage. For example, you might find that you test for an infection, #D-5. If the severity is 'light,' maybe all you need to do is rest, eat simply and take some vitamins. However, if you test for 'heavy' severity and your pendulum moves to the Red Flag, this may indicate that you need to get help and see a healthcare provider. As previously mentioned, common sense is a necessary part of being a good dowser.

White Flag: The use of the White Flag may indicate that there is more information available. You may have a question about a relationship and might ask "Which flag is dominant for me in this situation?" For example you have two possible date options and cannot decide who to go out with. See what your dowsing says.

You might also use this aspect of the chart for compatibility. It is wise to check for a benefit before attending a workshop, lecture or a public event. For instance, after testing whether it was beneficial to me, I declined to attend a talk upon invitation from a famous UFOlogist. Months later, after a personal exchange with the UFOlogist, I realized why there was no benefit to attend the lecture. He was leaning towards the dark side of the force and none of his predictions were ever accurate.

Light, Medium and Heavy: These should be self explanatory. If not, ask the question *"On a sliding scale of 1 to 10, what level or intensity is this?"* Trust your findings. Find your trusting. Use your higher mind and chakra system to get past a 3D reliance on your five senses. Get grounded in awareness and be open to your intuition.

Letters and Numbers: Use the numbers and letters in the chart to identify which section and which item in a section is positive. You can also use them to test for percentages.

The Invocations: These are statements that essentially prepare those involved for a dowsing session. They are most powerful and will assist you in clearing energy and in bringing in more light.

The Invocation

> *"I surround myself with a spinning column of white light, connecting one end to source and the other end to the healing temple at the center of the Earth. Now I invoke my mighty I AM Presence and the Violet Flame of Transmutation to completely over light my body and being; to align, clear, harmonize and balance my personal trinity; to clear my soul committee, guides and guardian angels, and to harmonize all with the divine plan."*

If you are absolutely new to dowsing but have a good heart and a clear intention you can, by utilizing the Invocations on the chart and the Clearing Macro, truly begin to transform your life, and those of your loved ones. Of course you can clear your boss, co-workers and even any adversaries (with permission) and eliminate some of those speed bumps in your path. How do you get permission? You ask a person's Higher Self: *"May I? Can I? Should I?"* and go or no.

This invocation on the chart is an abbreviated form of the "*I AM* Meditation" which is a 12-minute guided visualization invocation and meditation. You can access this for free at www.LifeSeedCodes.com and explore this music meditation for additional clearing and protection. The constructive use of violet flame visualization has a power that is most beneficial and is utilized in this meditation. The *I AM* is the God Spark within and is key to all our transformations and healings.

Clearing Macro: I wish to thank my teacher Carole Conlon for the loan of the Clearing Macro. This statement is the key to obtaining the best results to complete the clearing process; moving energies through the body, mind and spirit. Other charts fail to give a precise tool, intention or step for this action. When the Clearing Macro is recited as a focused sound intention, that wave of energy balances and neutralizes or clears energetic disturbances. I like to place my pendulum over the Clearing Macro, letting it spin in a clockwise direction while I recite the statement out loud.

Completion Check: By reading the completion check following a clearing, the dowser can be sure that an issue is totally cleared on all levels - the self, soul and ego - for a person being cleared. This also acts to double check that the clearing was thorough.

The Chart Sections: First I must say that this chart is always to be a work in progress. My primary interest here is to assist people to learn basic clearing techniques. Usually when people are having problems with one another, there are problems on the astral/energy level. My mantra is "as above, so below."

If you are absolutely new to dowsing but have a good heart and a clear intention you can, by utilizing the Invocations on the chart and the Clearing Macro, truly begin to transform your life, and those of your loved ones. Of course you can clear your boss, co-workers and even any adversaries (with permission) and eliminate some of those speed bumps in your path. How do you get permission? You ask a person's Higher Self: *"May I? Can I? Should I?"* and go or no.

Section Descriptions

SECTION A   Hitchhikers . . . Cords . . . Chakras

The reason why these three influences are placed together here is simply so the very absolute beginner can go through the process of *"May I? Can I? Should I?"* read the invocations (at least the first one to prepare for dowsing), ask a question, find an issue and then use the Clearing Macro. Your request to clear all the influences at the same time will be successful. Later after you have done more clearing work, go back and ask which one it was. But you can clear things quickly without going in depth. You will get results.

Hitchhiker's is a pleasant term used for entities/spirits/ghosts and these are found in large numbers on what is called the astral plane. When we sleep, we leave the body and travel through this astral level. If a person is deficient in spiritual strength, it is easy to bring back these very undesirable and invisible guests. It might even be possible to assign this value to them: All negative thought, emotion and actions are assisted by these entities that desire the status quo of chaos and negativity. Zero for the hero is best.

Cords are energetic attachments that flow either in or out of our energy fields. In our work, cords are considered to be energetic entanglements that flow in to us and limit and bind us physically, mentally and emotionally. People often attach cords to others in a most innocent subconscious way. But whether conscious or subconscious, intentional or not, cords are bad for the system and must be removed or one's energies will be severely drained. Cord is the term for inbound energy. Attachment is for the outbound.

Chakras are the internal energy centers located along the spine. It is commonly believed that there are seven major ones in number that work in an invisible way to collect subtle energy from our surroundings and distribute it throughout the body.

As you read further, you will notice that there is some intentional duplication from Section A with other sections. This is because it is very important to get Section A issues cleared. Also for the beginner, clearing Section A may be all you desire to do until positive personal evidence indicates and supports further inquiry and dedication. At this point, and with practice, your pendulum skills will begin to develop.

Without question, if a person would clear and balance themselves to where they had zero entities, zero cords and attachments and all chakras clear and balanced, they would function at a much more fluid and masterful capacity in life.

SECTION B
1. Electrical Energy (including Meridians and Related Circuitry)
2. Aura . . . Weak, Leaks, Damaged, Levels, Prana
3. Chakras . . . Balance, Color, Size, Shape
4. Vitality . . . Chi, Yin, Yang, Prana, Life Energies, Love
5. Shadow Energies . . . Home, Workplace, Other Space, Travel Places
6. Vitamins . . . A, B, C, D, E, etc.
7. Minerals . . . Magnesium, Calcium, etc.
8. Harmony . . . Rest, Sleep, Nutrition, Fluids, Salts, etc.

SECTION C
1. Mental . . . Control, Energies, Function, Balance, Stability, Projections
2. Emotion . . . Hormone, Environment, Substances (food, medicines, stimulants, etc.)
3. Image . . . Attitude about Life, People, World, Self, Success, Health
4. Programs . . . Patterns, Mindsets, Habits, Traits, Culture, Ancestral, Past Lives
5. Nervous System . . . Stress, Defects, Genetic, Energetic
6. Chaotic . . . Vibrations, Environment, Persons, Oppressions, Pressures
7. Draining of Energies . . . by any System, Person, Force, or Entities
8. Cords . . . Inbound or Outbound Attachments to others' Chakras or Anatomy
9. Ancestral . . . Past Life, Effects, Entanglements, Attachments, Karma
10. Hitchhikers . . . Astral Energies or Beings, Interfering, Obstructing
11. Influences . . . Combinations of Psychic, Emotional, Mental, Entanglements, Astral Influences, Entities, Karma, Environment

12. Protection . . . Weakness of Physical, Mental, Psychic, Astral, Aura, Influences, Energies, Forces, etc.

SECTION D
1. Ions and Electrolytes
2. Amino Acids . . . Levels, Balance
3. Acid/Alkaline
4. Toxins
5. Infections
6. Allergies . . . Plant, Animal, Chemical, Mental, Emotional, Psychic
7. Systems . . . Digestion, Circulation, Immune System, Hormone, Enzyme, Communication, etc.
8. Discomfort . . . Pain, Warning, Physical, Mental, Psychic, Spiritual, Astral
9. Pressures . . . Nerve, Structure, Fluid, Blood

Obviously for complete healing we may still require physical remedies for some of these categories but understand that most effects or symptoms have causes on the mental, emotional and other planes as well. This is why it is important to clear them through dowsing.

SECTION E   Beyond . . . and Outside the Box . . . Cause of situation is beyond our grasp

This section is an indicator that things beyond our normal degree of observation have come into play. These could be Earth, planetary or solar changes or any number of other influences. If I feel off balance and cannot find the influence in Sections A, B, C or D, then I will have to check Section E; and sometimes my pendulum will swing in a counterclockwise fashion, indicating that something is truly off the normal range and beyond my/our grasp. No you are not going crazy. Is it possible that the planet is moving into a higher dimension and experiencing birthing pains? Oh, yes!

SECTION F   Activities

In any given moment, as you begin to focus on the question of *"What is my highest option?"* the activities section becomes valuable. Since there are 12 options you must start with the pendulum in balance/neutral position. Ask the question, *"How many digits in the number?"* The correct answer will be one or two. A one digit means that your option can range from 1 to 9. If the answer is two digits, then your options are numbers 10, 11 or 12. To find out which number, dowse and get a #1, go back to neutral and dowse the second digit to get a 0, 1, or 2 (10, 11, 12 respectively). It is best when beginning to do work in this section that you follow the protocols of *"May I, Can I, Should I?"* and recite the Invocation. Be sure you are "in the clear."

SECTION G   Seven Chakras

This section is for checking in on the individual chakras. If you are not familiar with chakras, I recommend that you do some research. Using this chart, you can clear all of them at the same time as follows:

1. Recite the invocation and ask for permission to work *"May I, Can I, Should?"* (if you have not already done it for other testing)
2. Test if Ready
3. Ask: "Are my chakras all aligned, cleared, open and balanced?"
    o If 'yes', you are done.
    o If 'no', recite the clearing macro by *"bundling and spiraling all my chakras down through my body, mind and spirit. . . "*

Later, as we use the beginner's chart to advance our daily self analysis, we will want to start focusing more specifically by defining which chakras tend to stray out of alignment and balance.

SECTION H   Using the *I AM* Chart

The *I AM* chart brings in many positive elements and energies that can be infused into your being, including Colors, Affirmations, Positive Dispositions, Virtues,

Qualities of Heart Fullness, Archangels and Others to Call Upon when in need. This chart is detailed in Chapter Five.

SECTION I   Graduate to the LifeWeaving Charts

The two best resources for dowsing that I have found are Walt Woods and his "Letter to Robin" and, of course, Carole Conlon at AyniLifeWeaving.com. I met Walt Woods and he was a very happy type of gentlemen. Walt smiled a lot. He told us a story about going in to a hospital laboratory where he tested 10 people who were advanced dowsers. They were able to generate delta brain waves that were unlike anything the technician had ever seen in a person who was not in a coma. The basis for the Be Clear Now chart was inspired by Walt's work.

And of course we have Carole Conlon and the LifeWeaving charts and system. Carole's is the best, plain and simple.

Put your pendulum in a neutral swing and check to see when you may be ready to start using the LifeWeaving charts.

Source of Information

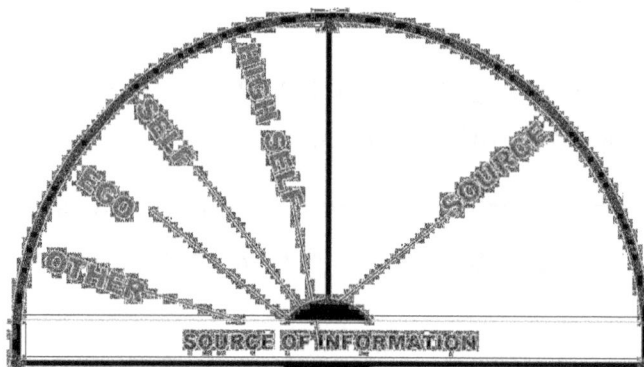

The Source of Information chart provides a quick way to test where the information you are receiving is coming from as you dowse. For simplicity, the goal is to only accept answers if they come from Source.

To use this chart:

1. Place your pendulum in a gentle swing along the vertical neutral line
2. Ask *"Who is this information coming from?"* Note: Always allow time for more than one answer, if there are any, as there could be a combination of ego and self, etc. If a situation like this arises, clear yourself with the Violet Flame Invocation and retest.
3. If information is coming only from Source, all is good.
4. Information coming from any combination of other, ego, self or high self with or without Source cannot be trusted. Reaffirm you are only accepting answers from Source. If you cannot clear this, stop and try later.

Now that you've met the Be Clear Now chart, it's time to dive in and start dowsing.

[3]

Using the Be Clear Now Chart

To dig deeper into the mystery of *"Am I in balance?"* is to put your pendulum in a neutral swing and go through the following procedure.

Be Clear Now Dowsing Steps

1. Recite the Invocation to prepare for work, ending with the all important *"May I, Can I, Should I?"*

2. Put the pendulum in motion (North to South swing) in the Balance zone and ask, *"Am I Ready to begin?"*
   - If the pendulum moves to the green Ready diamond, continue to the next step.
   - If the pendulum does not indicate 'Ready', repeat steps #1 & 2 until Ready is indicated or just stop trying for the time being.

3. Put the pendulum in motion (North to South swing) and ask, *"Am I in balance?"*
   - If the pendulum goes to the "YES" circle, congratulations! You are balanced and your session is complete.
   - If the pendulum goes to the "NO" circle, continue to step #4.

4. Go back to Balance with your pendulum and ask *"What section needs clearing?"* Find which letter J - A.

5. Go back to Balance again and ask *"What number in that section?"* Find #1-10.

6. (Optional) You can also ask, *"What is the level in effect for this section?"* Find light-medium-heavy.

7. (Optional) After you identify the letter and number you can check the section description keys to see what exactly is being cleared.

8. To complete the clearing, place the pendulum over the Clearing Macro and repeat the Mantra: *"I bundle and spiral all words, ideas and energies associated with Section ___ through my body, mind and spirit at all body levels, frequencies, realities, incarnations, dimensions and for all times; plus all blocks, memories, intent and healing. Now I flood with unconditional love to fill in where energy has been removed."* (Let your pendulum continue spinning for as long as is necessary.)

9. Go back to Balance and recheck that your pendulum remains in Balance/Neutral for the section and number you just cleared before moving on to your next question. Ask *"Am I in balance?"* Continue testing as needed.

10. Repeat steps 1-10 until your pendulum remains at Balance, indicating no further problems or issues to clear at this time.

[4]

Be Clear Now! Stories

A Story About Cording

My friend Sonya S. (blessings be upon her sweet soul) was called to travel to Germany from Seattle due to the death of her stepmother. She was the only living relative of this woman. The lady, a bad ombre, was mean and caused Sonja nothing but heartache throughout her whole life. She is the reason Sonja had left Germany, trying to get away from the dense energies and hoping for better times here in the United States.

So Sonja boarded a flight from Seattle to Germany the day after the wicked stepmother died. But when her flight touched down in Germany she experienced temporary blindness. She contacted me by phone.

I assessed that she had been attacked by the stepmother as she was pulled back into that energy. I personally had never seen a situation like this. I did as much as I could and eventually after months of treatment her vision was restored. This was a deal breaker for me. I thought I was a little crazy when I shared my dowsing results with Sonja. Very much to my surprise, she fully and completely agreed with me and was quite relieved that at least one person thought what she thought and felt what she felt about this attack.

I personally believe that we as a people need to "Be Clear Now" and vibrate a love and light frequency so that we can float above the turbulence. A person who has no baggage, cellular memory, unhealed business is not likely to be affected by a psychic attack in the same way. Invoke the light every day. It works!

A Story About A Curse

A friend of mine (J.J.) moved back in with her aging mother to help look after her. During that same time her mom had a problem with a road at her house that was common property with the neighbor. A construction project was bringing some trucks by the house and causing some dust to blow. The mom was angry about it, always yelling that she was going to put a spell on the truck driver if he continued to drive the road. I was clearing J.J. and assisting her with a constant cord problem (another story), but one day I decided to look in on (dowse) mom. I was very surprised to find that mom had some curse spell energy attached to her. Who would want to put some voodoo on a nice little old lady like her?

That is when J.J. told me the story.

When I spoke to J.J. about my findings, she told me about the mom sending out spell energy at the truck driver. She laughed, truly amazed at the findings, and went on to become a very proficient LifeWeaver, and is still learning. Aren't we all?

And mom hopefully learned a lesson about how spells and curses tend to boomerang back to the sender!

Have More Compassion and Be Slow to Criticize

Don't be normal, be a miracle

The Course in Miracles says that when a miracle is not happening, then something is wrong. It also explains states of awareness and experience as opportunity to transcend the normal laws of physics. For example, when love is present it blesses both the giver and the receiver. The new normal needs to be this possibility, dignity, and courtesy and love if you can get there. Knowing what not to do, can also be as vital as knowing what to do. One can paint over a thing we have said to a person but we never can take it back.

I was sitting with my guitar one morning and I kept getting distracted by a picture in my mind's eye of Tom Cruise and Brad Pitt from the movie *An Interview with a Vampire*. It was a strange image for sure. I do not consider myself a clairvoyant by any means, but everyone has got a third (inner) eye. Because of that third eye, I decided to get out the charts and see if this was a warning about my next client's energy.

It definitely was.

Funny thing is that my client is a minister/astrologer and a very sweet and a well-meaning person. I discovered while dowsing that she had a sufficient amount of entities and other energetic disturbances. So I facilitated the clearing before she arrived. After she arrived and got settled in, I shared my discovery with her. She expressed that the previous day she had laid into her husband big time, screaming so loud that he had to put his fingers in his ears. Now please realize that blasting someone like that creates holes in your aura and immediately invites in the bad beings from the astral plane — the spooks, entities, and hitchhikers. Got it!

Reporting our findings is an art that develops right at the speed of our own compassion, and not a bit sooner. I was very surprised when she told me about the exchange with her husband but I did not let her know this. People can police themselves. All they need sometimes is the clear mirror, one that has been polished with compassion. Be gentle with discovery with folks. Sometimes you can just do a clearing and not say a thing. Yes, we are all integrating this one.

Personal Observations About Doing Clearing Work

If absence makes the heart grow fonder I wonder how silence affects us? It gives us more time to stay out of duality for sure. Usually when I am clearing for another person I am doing it alone in a quiet space. Other times I work in concert with my partner Karin and this is truly fun and powerful. The balance of male and female energy can be just the miracle you want, to add that dynamic harmony into a session.

The work we do together is Diamond Heart Energy Activations. More information can be found at the end of this book.

I am working with clearing, integration and activation and that is it. Karin and I have been doing clearing on a gentleman every day for 3 to 4 weeks. Today he told his wife he was going into Alcoholics Anonymous. Now we never discussed alcohol while working with him; we just kept clearing the entities. Now he is on his own initiative and moving forward. That is what I love about "the system" of dowsing. Every day is a miracle.

There is great work happening on many levels and many great people doing it, yourself very much so.

A Family Restored: Release the Blocks and Entities, Bring on Transformation

I think that because I have a background in healing in general and self-healing in particular, I have found that it is especially challenging to work with people not at least somewhat engaged in their own healing work.

Some years ago a family member asked me to do the Be Clear Now work for them and a significant other, who had an entity problem. I remember that having to always clear them was not really exciting at all. I did work with them for 2½ weeks before encouraging them to get up to speed with their own clearing work. I was done.

However, recently I was put into a situation where I had to dig in and assist an individual who, up until now, had not demonstrated any interest in my work or any interest in anything even remotely spiritual. Again, I found it hard for me to do this work which was ongoing for months. Today I learned that this individual has joined Alcoholics Anonymous and even had the courage to tell his partner that he has begun the healing.

All I did was clearing work every day. Part of this clearing and energizing work included reading the *Pattern on the Trestleboard* out loud as an *"I AM"* invocation for this person. I also requested that the individual memorize this. Why memorize? Because, memorization embeds the words into the subconscious mind. Also, after it is memorized, the words become a great mantra to do when chaos, fear or worldly indifference seems to want to run a number on you.

The *Pattern on the Trestleboard* can be found in Appendix III, page 41.

Being part of this experiment has been very rewarding to me. As mentioned previously, up until this time I have personally been in resistance to working for under-motivated people. Now I see more proof and another demonstration of how powerful "clearing" work can be. People will receive the energy and eventually get up and move for themselves; marriages are renewed and families restored. I originally agreed to do this work for the benefit of the couple's children whose picture sits above my charts. Soon I can replace it with a photo of the whole family.

Do the work, and get the results.

My Experience with the Chart Invocations

The magic of invocations is that they are powerful tools. Found in all the cultures of the world, invocations help one to gain access to the vibrations, energy and frequencies of the higher dimensions as well as higher aspects of our own being. As a child I used to like to go into a church and just sit. My home life was rough. I was beaten up regularly by an older brother and by my father. I knew that in that quiet space of the church I could sit for a few minutes and let my guard down. I had great experiences in this place. One time as a boy all of twelve years of age, I walked into a church at 6:15 A.M. I was the only one there and with all those lit candles, I felt the energy of a higher world. It was pure and rich without any of the chaos of people, place and things.

I have explored the spiritual sciences of the Hindus, Seiks, Sufis, Buddhists, Taoists, Islam and Christians. They are all beautiful branches of a tree that share the same roots. Did you know that there are over 2000 names for the Divine Mother in Hinduism? That the Muslims have 99 names for Allah? That Christians have a saint for most things (Saint Christopher is a great saint for protection while traveling)? I am not certain that one name has more power than another, but I am certain that when invoked with sincerity, any and all names will produce a frequency that is harmonious to the mind, body and spirit.

The invocations work like that, producing a frequency conducive for clearing. Be sure to use them in your work.

[5]

The *I AM* Chart

The *I AM* Chart and this aspect of the book is bonus material. I did not want to put the burden of another purchase on anyone so I am giving you this opportunity to focus and to send these healing energies, found on the chart, to those who are already comfortable, familiar and ready with concepts around "lightworking." You can certainly "Be Clear Now" without this section.

What I also recommend is that you experiment with the *I AM* Meditation on the web site **LifeSeedCodes.com**. It is FREE.

Now the *I AM* is the name for our permanent Atom of Self. It is our real and true nature and the place from where we launch into experience or lifetimes, for the purpose of soul development. From a place of original innocence we volunteered for the job. Now we have to get back to the garden. Remember that your personality is just the clothes you wear for this journey; you are not your horoscope. You are made of star stuff and that's a fact. The *I AM* Presence is that fact but beyond the conscious mind's ability to fully grasp. It is fully pristine I am told, and our personality, our body and the total contents of our personal lives are microscopic in comparison to our Real and True Self or *I AM* Presence. I think of it as though our Presence sends out a "thread" into the place of space and time for the expressed purpose of becoming a co-creator, to get the bumps and learn the ropes. We need to co-create together as well, with each other. For me, creating this book is an opportunity to work with my partner Karin for the art. We are more powerful together.

Why the *I AM* Chart Came into Existence

After many years of working in the healing arts in too many systems to mention, and with my studies and application of the LifeWeaving system, it became very clear to me that thoughts have real substance on the mental plane. The fields in which our beings live and move are alive with vitality. They are alive and respond to our thoughts. You can easily download, say, "compassion", by setting the intent and making the request. So as I was clearing all the negative imprints with the Be Clear Now method, I felt a need to focus in a more dynamic fashion with positive qualities of light in the form of Virtues, Affirmations, Mindful Attitudes, Positive Dispositions and more. So once again with the assistance of our dear Carole Conlon, we came up with a chart for just this purpose: to send those good qualities to the people we are working with.

I AM Chart Sections

Invocation: This statement is used to clear the person you are working on if you have not already done so as part of a clearing session.

In preparation for dowsing ask:
May I? Can I? Should I?
NO? (Stop). YES? (Do the invocation and
then go to the Chart Key to dowse.)

INVOCATION
I surround myself with a spinning column of white light,
connecting one end to Unlimited Source and the other
to the Healing Temple at the center of the Earth.
Now I invoke my mighty I AM presence and the Violet Flame of Transmutation
to completely over light my body and being,
To align, clear, harmonize and balance my personal Trinity,
To clear soul committee, guides and guardian angels,
and to harmonize all with the Divine Plan.

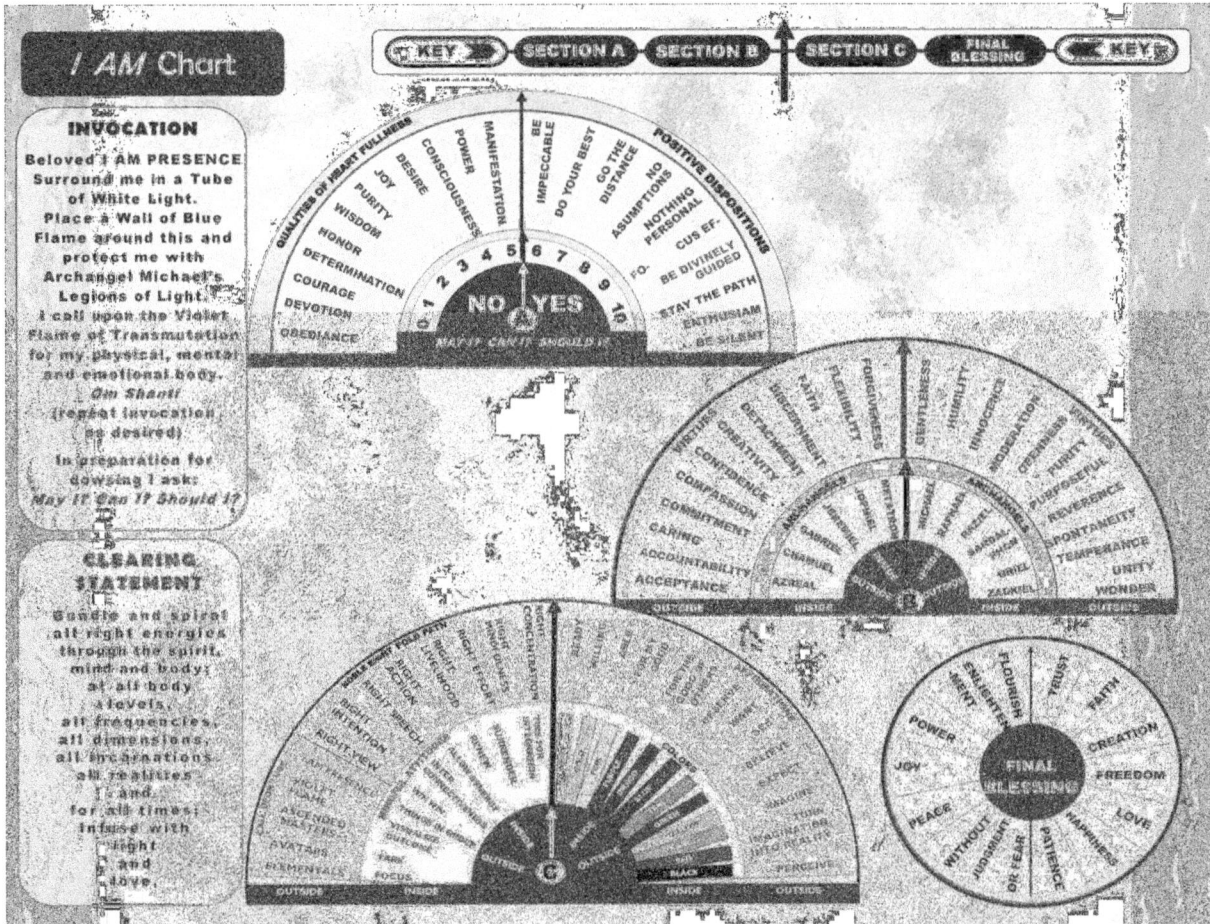

The *I AM* Chart

Chart Key: The Chart Key is always dowsed first. It allows you to go immediately to any pertinent sections of the chart (A, B, C or the Final Blessing) that hold information for you or your client.

Section A
- Qualities of Heart Fullness
- Positive Dispositions
- Numbers

- No/Yes

SECTION A

To Test Section A:

1. Begin on the Section A Neutral Line
2. Ask your yes-no or number question and see what comes up; OR
3. Ask what quality or positive disposition would be helpful.

Section B

- Virtues
- Archangels

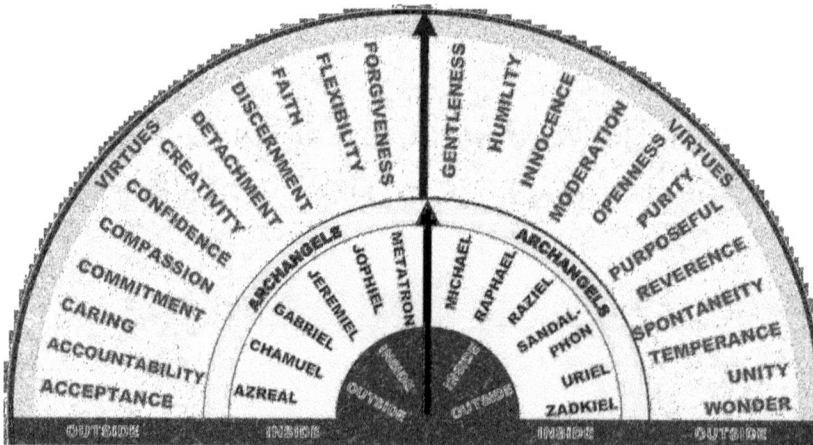

SECTION B

To Test Section B:

1. Begin dowsing with your pendulum in a neutral swing on the Section B Neutral Line
2. Dowse the inner circle of the section to see if you are reading the inside or outside row of answers.
3. Find the words for that section, allowing for more than one answer, if there are any.
4. Your pendulum returns to the neutral line when the section is complete. (Train it to do this motion.)

Section C

- Call Upon/Use
- Noble Eight Fold Path
- Affirmations
- Mindful Attitudes
- Colors

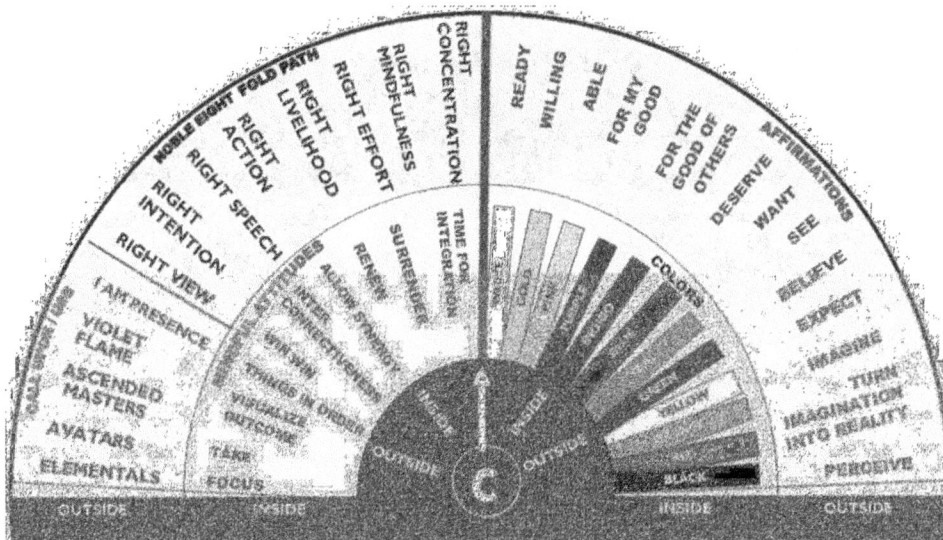

SECTION C

To Test Section C

1. Begin on the Section C Neutral Line.

2. Dowse the inside circle of the section to see if you should read the inside or outside row of answers.
3. Place your attention on the indicated row and find any answers. (Allow for more than one answer if there are any.)
4. Your pendulum returns to the section neutral line when all words have been found.

Final Blessing

The final Blessing is a high vibrational prayer that can be dowsed to find specific words to enhance healing.

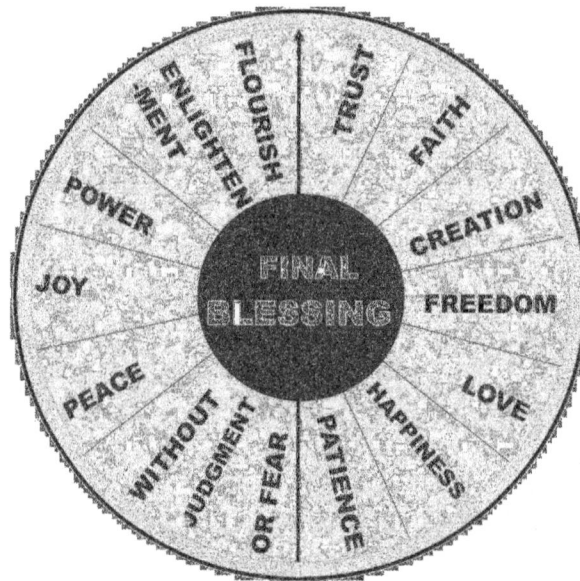

FINAL BLESSING

To test the Final Blessing Chart
1. Begin on the neutral line of this circular chart
2. Let your pendulum select all the qualities that need to be added. Note, if your pendulum spins in a circle over this section, simply ask to add all the words in.

Note that working with a circular chart requires that you know what the 'leading edge' of the pendulum swing is (the portion moving away from you) so you know whether to read a word at the top of the circular chart or the word found opposite it at the bottom of the circle. If you are not sure of what the leading edge of your pendulum is, or to avoid confusion, you can also ask *"Which side of the chart should I read — left or right side?"* Then ask to see the word or words on the indicated side of the chart.

Clearing Statement: As you test for qualities on the *I AM* Chart, mentally drop them into an imaginary basket until you have completed this section. Then, using the Clearing Statement, spiral them all down through the person being worked on. As they spiral, they will be retained by the body and assist healing.

Using the *I AM* Chart

1. Place your pendulum on the Chart Key neutral line in a gentle neutral swing
2. Ask to see which section to test first.
3. Beginning on the neutral line of the section that just tested, dowse for answers while allowing for more than one item to come up at a time (if there are more than one).
4. Send the words that have dowsed down through the person being tested. You can visualize spiraling them down through body, mind and spirit while reading the clearing statement. [Optional: use an imaginary basket to collect all the words as you test a section of the chart; then when testing is complete, read the Clearing Statement found on the *I AM* Chart.]
5. When your pendulum returns to the neutral line of the section you are on, it indicates that the section is complete. (Note that often you need to 'train' your pendulum to make this move.)
6. Return to the Chart Key neutral line
7. Ask to see the next section to test (if any).

8. Continue steps 1 - 7 until your pendulum remains on the neutral line of the Chart Key, indicating completion.

9. Read the Clearing Statement to complete your session if you haven't cleared each section as you worked.

[6]
Now It's Time to Practice

Now that you know the basics of pendulum clearing, the next step is to keep practicing! Some people find dowsing easy while others have definite blocks. In my experience, blocks usually test due to your guardian angels preventing you from dowsing because pendulum usage got you into trouble in a past life. So promise your angels that you will only work for good this time around or demand that those angels *"Be cleared, removed or replaced as needed"* to allow you to be able to dowse.

Above all, keep yourself clear by working on yourself every day and enjoy a new bright life.

Appendix I
The Reset Exercise

Dear Anyone and/or Everyone,

If I have compromised you, or caused you harm, in any way possible, either for real or imagined, in this life or any other life, in this dimension or any other dimension, I humbly apologize to you. I ask for your complete forgiveness here and now.

And, I forgive you likewise.

Also I release myself from having to contribute to your well being in all ways unless you specifically ask. I am here to work on myself!

And, I release you likewise.

You are a great human being. We have the same Creator.

I AM perusing my destiny and completion with planet Earth and its fine people. *I AM* returning home, in LIGHT fashion.

You are completely excused from having to either understand or appreciate what this means to ME.

There is no assessment or validation that you have to make about my decisions. You are free to move forward respectfully!

You may choose to ask God or not, what the plan for me is. I am in partnership with Her!

I am finished explaining myself! I am finished trying to explain myself!

I AM not a victim in any way shape or form. I accept responsibility for what I attract in my life; therefore, I reserve this right for myself and for you!

If I feel, intuit or observe in any way that you or any other person is compromised by blocks, blindness, cords, distortions, entities, karma, cooties, crap, time capsules, openings, spiral tracks, thought forms, trauma imprints, gas or any other condition: I reserve the right to head for the hills. I support OUR Freedom to Choose!

My moment of Now is Sacred and Self-sustaining. It has a future pull and so it does NOT require any traction from any past, whatever reality, idea, dream or nightmare it may be.

I AM a heart-centered being of Light on Purpose, I AM sending out a blessing to all life! Not because (state your name) is, was, or will continue to be, but simply because, *I AM.*

I AM here and now re-setting my goals, practice and orientation for ALL my relationships. All cords are cut and, only heartstrings need apply.

Namáste!

Appendix II
Namáste Re-Set Exercise

After reading the Re-Set Exercise out loud the Namáste greeting brings more emotion to the surface, tears of joy and laughter of release.

We have experimented with going around the room and having each person who wishes to, to read a sentence of the Re-Set out loud. This charges the room with a larger than individual intent and promotes a group chemistry.

Namáste is a greeting from heart to heart.

Namáste is the recognition that God stuff abides here.

Namáste transcends the flesh to the Spirit of Fellowship and the Heart of Belonging.

Namáste is this flow of a finer wave of the lightness of Being.

Let each person who is present and who cares to participate, simply move around the room and do the Namáste blessing, hands across the heart, for one another. Allow enough time for each person to Namáste all they like. Then allow time for integration.

Namáste

Appendix III
The Pattern on the Trestleboard

This Is Truth About The Self

0. All the Power that ever was or will be is here now.

1. I am a center of expression for the Primal Will-to-Good which eternally creates and sustains the Universe.

2. Through me its unfailing Wisdom takes form in thought and word.

3. Filled with Understanding of its perfect law, I am guided, moment by moment, along the path of liberation.

4. From the exhaustless riches of its Limitless Substance, I draw all things needful, both spiritual and material.

5. I recognize the manifestation of the Undeviating Justice in all the circumstances of my life.

6. In all things, great and small, I see the Beauty of the Divine Expression.

7. Living from that Will, supported by its unfailing Wisdom and Understanding, mine is the Victorious Life.

8. I look forward with confidence to the perfect realization of the Eternal Splendor of the Limitless Light.

9. In thought and word and deed, I rest my life, from day to day, upon the sure Foundation of Eternal Being.

10. The Kingdom of Spirit is embodied in my flesh.

Meet the Author

Brian T Roberts

Ambassador of LifeSeed
Developer of the Diamond Heart Energy Activations
Doctor of Divinity / Minister
Licensed Massage Practitioner
Musician / Song Writer / Performer
Sacred Ceremonialist

Brian Roberts, a licensed health care professional since 1976, graduated from three Florida schools for massage and body work in the late seventies. His career and personal development has involved ongoing studies in holistic or mind-body-spirit approaches. After completing studies and initiation in meditation from various disciplines, Brian moved on to the study of Body Centered Psychotherapy utilizing principals of Buddhism, Taoism, non-violence and unity for his healing and counseling work.

In 1992 Brian returned to Seattle to continue studies in hypnosis, meditation and Alphabiotics, an off-shoot of chiropractic medicine which works specifically with the synchronization of the left and right brain hemispheres. During the next ten years Brian maintained a busy Alphabiotic Alignment practice and continued studies in nutrition, Contact Reflex Analysis and Bija Meditation. During this time he also made visits to the Far East where he was initiated as a Babaji Bija Meditation Initiate with the Council of Light.

Also during this period as a minister, he facilitated study groups in *A Course in Miracles* and conducted over one thousand ceremonies which included weddings, christenings, memorials and meditation initiations.

Today Brian maintains the Lifeseed wellness practice, and conducts a weekly meditation and Lifeseed development circle.

Ask and you shall receive.
Seek and you will find.
Knock and the doors will be open to you.

Remember to ask, *"May I? Can I? Should I?"*

Dowsing is not supernatural, mystical or magical but is rather the expansion of one's common sense.

Good dowsing, everyone!

Diamond Heart Energy Activation Offer from Brian Roberts

In my book, *I AM* Presence, Diamond Heart Energy Activations, I take people through 12 unique meditations accompanied by music, making a very focused attempt to assist people in developing this connection. One of these meditations, the 12 minute *I AM* meditation, is available for download on my website LifeSeedCodes.com.

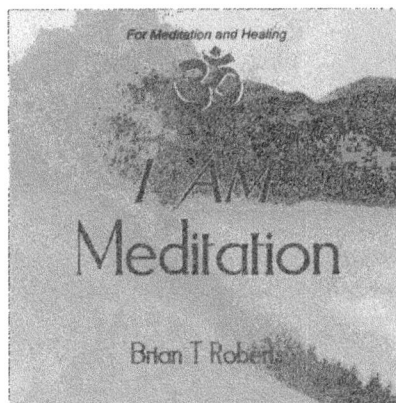

Oh, and did I mention that it is FREE?

Try this *I AM* meditation and if you resonate with it, I suggest that you get the book and access to all 12 Activations. They will help you immensely in getting into the energies of the *I AM* chart. I want you to be powerful. As all good things flow downward from above, and from inside to outside, these activations set up the necessary energetic patterns to master this flow.

There is only One mind and we are all tapping into it. We can definitely have a positive impact on a person, place or thing from any distance by entering into the right consciousness. We can do this from Unity consciousness, from the *I AM*. We can use the chart, flow the energies, feel the energies and have an impact on the world around us. Amen!

LifeWeaving Information

If you are ready for the next step in clearing, you can find more information at AyniLifeWeaving.com. Be sure to check out the videos on the website that show how these unique charts are used. LifeWeaving books and charts are also available at either AyniLifeWeaving.com or Amazon.com.

LIFEWEAVING CHARTS

REMEMBER!

FOR YOUR FREE PDF files of the Be Clear Now and I AM charts, send an email request to brianrobertsbodywork@gmail.com or use the contact form at AyniWritePress.com.

---

www.ingramcontent.com/pod-product-compliance
Lightning Source LLC
LaVergne TN
LVHW061229060426
835509LV00012B/1479